Adobe InCopy Tutorial Guide

The Definitive User Manual To Master
InCopy with Illustrations

By

Isaac Alejo

Table of Content

Table of Content 2

Introduction 5

Chapter 1: Workspace 6

Workspace Basics 6

Workspace overview 6

Hide or show all panels 8

Reconfigure the Tools panel 8

Viewing Stories 9

Galley, Story, and Layout view overview 9

Customize Galley and Story views 13

View documents 16

Moving Through Documents 20

Scrolling through documents 20

Move through a document with the Hand tool. 20

Jump to position markers. 21

Reorder InCopy stories 22

Recovery and Undo 22

Recover documents 22

Undo mistakes 25

Customizing Preferences and Defaults 25

Set defaults 26

Specify default settings for new objects in a document ... 27

Chapter 2: InCopy documents 29

Transforming Graphics 29

Position tool overview 29

Transform graphics 30

Stand-Alone Documents 33

Work with stand-alone documents. 33

Using Adobe Bridge with InCopy 36

Saving and Exporting 37

Save documents 37

Export InCopy documents 40

Rename InCopy stories 43

Export content to Buzzword 43

Importing Graphics 44

Import graphics 44

Controlling Graphics Display 48

Control graphics' display performance 48

Chapter 3: Text 54

Adding Text 54

Importing files 55

Place (import) text 56

Import options 59

Import Buzzword documents 65

Type Asian text using inline input 67

Checking Spelling 68

To configure spelling preferences 69

To initiate a spell check 70

Correct spelling errors as you type 72

Use dynamic spelling 74

Editing Text 77

Paste text 77

Apply grid format to text...................................... 81

Change the text direction 81

Drag and drop text 81

Transpose characters 84

Edit text on a parent page 84

Undo actions 85

Find/Change..86

Find and change text...86

Conclusion **90**

INTRODUCTION

A dobe InCopy is a professional software developed by Adobe Inc. that collaborates with Adobe InDesign. It serves general word processing purposes, in contrast to InDesign, which focuses on publishing printed content like magazines. InCopy facilitates writing, editing, and designing documents.

Its workflows permit concurrent work on the same InDesign document, making it useful for teamwork. With its robust capabilities and integration with Adobe apps, InCopy is essential for enhancing workflow efficiency for writers, editors, and designers.

In this guide, we'll dive into the features of Adobe InCopy. Whether you're new or experienced, you'll learn about creating workflows, applying styles, and more. We'll also address advanced topics like automation and Adobe app integration to elevate your productivity.

Throughout the guide, we'll offer practical instances and step-by-step guidance to master InCopy. You'll acquire efficiency tips and techniques too. By the guide's end, you'll grasp InCopy thoroughly and understand its transformative potential for working with documents.

So, whether you're a writer, editor, or designer aiming to optimize workflow and productivity, this guide is tailored for you. Join us as we uncover the capabilities of Adobe InCopy.

CHAPTER 1: WORKSPACE

Workspace Basics

Workspace overview

The manipulation and creation of documents and files involve various components like panels, bars, and windows. Any arrangement of these components constitutes a workspace. Across different applications in Adobe® Creative Suite® 5, the workspaces share a uniform appearance, facilitating seamless transition between applications. Customization is also possible by selecting from preset workspaces or creating personalized ones to match your working preferences.

While the default layout of workspaces differs in various products, the manipulation of components remains consistent across all:

- The Application bar at the top features a workspace switcher, menus, and other application controls. On Mac, specific products can be shown or hidden using the Window menu.
- The Tools panel contains tools for image creation, artwork editing, page element manipulation, etc., with related tools grouped.
- The Control panel presents options for the currently selected tool or object (Illustrator) or the Options bar (Photoshop), Property Inspector (Flash, Dreamweaver, Fireworks) displaying properties of the current element.
- The Document window showcases the active file. It can be tabbed and, in specific cases, grouped and docked.
- Panels aid in monitoring and modifying work, like the Flash Timeline, Illustrator's Brush panel, Photoshop's Layers panel, or Dreamweaver's CSS Styles panel.
- The Application frame amalgamates all workspace elements into one integrated window, treating the application as a unified unit. Adjusting the frame or its elements causes them to respond in tandem, avoiding overlap. Panels remain visible when switching apps or clicking outside. For multitasking, you can arrange apps side by side on the screen or multiple monitors.

On a Mac, if you prefer the traditional user interface, you can deactivate the Application frame.

For instance, in Adobe Illustrator®, go to window> Application Frame to toggle it. (Flash on Mac has a permanent Application frame, while Dreamweaver for Mac lacks one.)

Hide or show all panels

- Press the Tab key to toggle the visibility of all panels, encompassing the Tools panel and Control panel.
- (Illustrator, InCopy, InDesign, Photoshop) Use Shift+Tab to conceal or reveal all panels except the Tools and Control panels.

  You can temporarily unveil hidden panels by activating Auto-Show Hidden Panels in Interface preferences. In Illustrator, this feature is always enabled. Hover your pointer over the application window's edge (Windows®) or the monitor's edge (Mac OS®) and rest it on the materialized strip.

- (Flash, Dreamweaver, Fireworks) Press F4 to hide or show all panels.

Reconfigure the Tools panel

In the Tools panel, you can arrange the tools in either a singular column or side by side in two columns. (This capability isn't present in the Fireworks and Flash Tools panel.)

Moreover, in InDesign and InCopy, you can transition between single-column and double-column (or single-row) layouts by adjusting a setting in Interface preferences. Click on the double arrow positioned at the top of the Tools panel.

Viewing Stories

Galley, Story, and Layout view overview

InCopy presents three perspectives for viewing a story: Galley, Story, and Layout. These terms mirror the language used in conventional publishing.

Galley view: Presents text with line breaks conforming to the corresponding Adobe InDesign® document layout. If the text exceeds the designated space, an overset indicates where the InCopy text extends beyond.

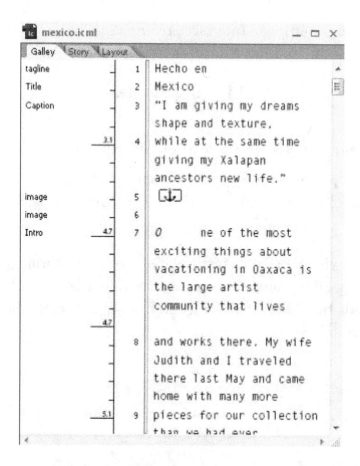

While you can apply formatting in InCopy, like paragraph indents and font size, these formats do not appear in the Galley view.

Story view: Shows text as a continuous stream, wrapping text within the document window. It doesn't show precise line endings, allowing you to focus on content. Nonetheless, if text surpasses the layout space, an overset indicator marks the point of excess. In the Story view, the information area exclusively displays paragraph styles, and line numbers remain concealed.

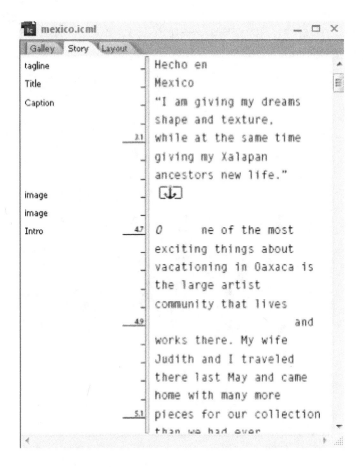

Upon creating a new InCopy story, Story view is the default.

To modify the default view for new documents, close all documents and select your desired default view from the View menu.

Layout view: Presents text in its print format, complete with all formatting. When synchronizing InCopy with an InDesign layout, you can observe text in conjunction with other page elements in the InDesign document—such as frames, columns, graphics, and more.

Switch between Galley, Story, or Layout view

To switch between galley, story, and layout view. Use one of the following:

- Choose the view from the View menu.

- Click the Galley, Story, or Layout tab at the top of the editing area.

Customize Galley and Story views

Galley and Story views can be customized in a variety of ways.

Change the Galley view display settings

- Choose a choice within the Galley & Story Appearance toolbar. (If this toolbar is concealed, access it by selecting Window > Galley & Story Appearance. By default, the toolbar emerges at the application window's lower section.)

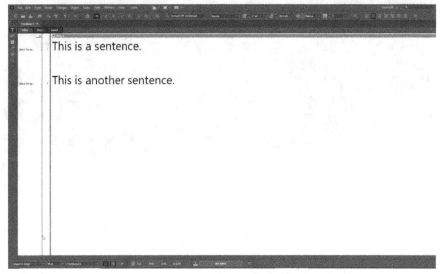

- Please understand the contrast between adjusting the font display size and implementing text formatting.
- Both actions can be executed in the Galley view. Modifying the font display size doesn't impact how text

appears in a publication, while applying text formatting alters text presentation in both the Layout view and the final published document.

Set Galley view display preferences

- Opt for Edit > Preferences > Galley & Story Display on Windows or InCopy > Preferences > Galley & Story Display on Mac OS.

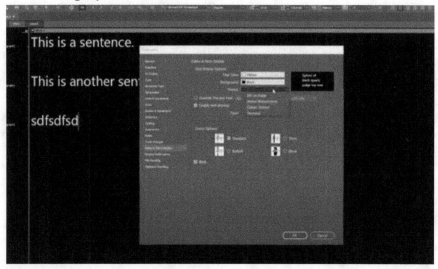

- Within the Text Display Options segment, define the following:
    1. **Text Color:** Manages the text color in the viewing area, with black as the default.
    2. **Background:** Dictates the background color of the viewing area, with white as the default backdrop.
    3. **Theme:** Assigns preconfigured text and background colors.

14

4. **Override Preview Font:** Allows an additional font to be shown correctly in the Galley and Story view, apart from the chosen display font. InCopy accurately displays Symbol, Zapf Dingbats, Webdings, and Wingdings® fonts, taking precedence over your chosen display font.

5. **Enable Anti-aliasing:** Smoothens jagged edges of text and bitmap images by gently transitioning color between edge and background pixels. This process maintains detail by altering only edge pixels. Different anti-aliasing levels are available. The Default option uses gray tones to refine the text. The LCD Optimized option utilizes colors instead of gray tones and works well with light backgrounds and black text. The Soft option employs gray tones but produces a softer, lighter appearance.

6. **Cursor Options:** Manages cursor display, offering four cursor choices. You can toggle the blink feature on or off.

Please note that any adjustments made in the Galley & Story Display section apply to both Galley and Story views.

Show or hide the information column
The info column is in Galley and Story views on the document window's left side. It presents non-editable details about paragraph styles, line numbers, and the vertical extent of text, making it an area where you can't input text.

Select one of these options:

- Pick View> Show Info Column or View > Hide Info Column to alter the View solely in the ongoing document.
- To modify the application's default view, close all documents and select View> Show Info Column or View > Hide Info Column.

View documents

Use the Zoom tool or View options to zoom in on or out of documents.

Zoom in or out

In the Layout view, you can adjust the page's scale, making it larger or smaller. The zoom percentage is exhibited on the application bar.

Here are a few actions you can take:

- To magnify a particular area, utilize the Zoom tool and click on the designated zone for magnification. Each click increases the view to the subsequent predetermined percentage, placing the display's center on the clicked point. When at maximum magnification, the center of the Zoom tool will be empty. To zoom out, hold Alt (Windows) or Option (Mac OS) to activate the Zoom Out tool, then click the area you wish to shrink. Each click reduces the view to the previous preset percentage.

- Enact the desired window and opt for view> Zoom In to enlarge the view to the following predetermined percentage. Choose view> Zoom Out to reduce the view to the earlier preset percentage.
- To establish a precise scale level, input or select a magnification value in the Zoom box within the application bar.
- While pressing Alt (Windows) or Option (Mac OS), use the mouse scroll wheel or sensor to zoom in or out.
- Use the Zoom tool or View options to zoom in on or out of documents.

Use Power Zoom

Power Zoom provides a rapid method to navigate your document's pages. By using the grabber hand, you can both zoom in or out and scroll across the entirety of your document. This feature proves especially advantageous for managing lengthy documents.

It's necessary to be in Layout view to employ power zoom.

- Click the Hand tool.
- With the grabber hand activated, click and keep the mouse button pressed.

The document will zoom out, offering a broader perspective of the spread. A red box denotes the visible area.

- While still holding down the mouse button, drag the red box to scroll through the document's pages. Use the arrow keys or the mouse scroll wheel to modify the red box's size.

- Release the mouse button to zoom in on the new portion of the document.
- The document window reverts to its initial zoom percentage or the dimensions of the red box.

Magnify by dragging

1. Choose the Zoom tool.
2. Drag your cursor to highlight the section you wish to enlarge.

3. To switch to the Zoom In tool while using a different tool, press Ctrl+spacebar (Windows) or Command+spacebar (Mac OS). To switch to the Zoom Out tool while using another tool, press Ctrl+Alt+spacebar (Windows) or Command+Option+spacebar (Mac OS).

Display the document at 100%
- Double-click the Zoom tool.
- Choose View > Actual Size.
- Choose a magnification level of 100% in the Zoom box in the application bar.

Fit the page, spread, or pasteboard within the active window
- Choose View > Fit Page In Window.
- Choose View > Fit Spread In Window.
- Choose View > Entire Pasteboard.

Moving Through Documents

Scrolling through documents

You have various methods to navigate through your content. You can use the scroll bars positioned along the bottom and right sides of the InCopy window or opt to scroll via a mouse wheel or sensor in any view.

Alternatively, you can rely on the keyboard's Page Up, Page Down, and arrow keys to traverse a story. The Page Up or Down keys shift to the next or previous page in the Layout view. In Galley or Story view, these keys adjust the view by one screen; it doesn't necessarily move to the next page break. The Up Arrow and Down Arrow keys shift the insertion point within the text and adjust the view to ensure the insertion point remains visible.

Solely within Layout view, you can utilize the Hand tool to shift the document view in any direction.

Move through a document with the Hand tool.

Different ways to navigate within a story vary based on whether you're in a Galley, Story, or Layout view. For Galley and Story views, you rely on the scroll bars to access text beyond the visible area. In the Layout view, additional methods like the Hand tool, page buttons, and specific commands come into play.

In the Layout view, opt for the Hand tool, then move the document by dragging it.

Jump to position markers.

You can establish a marker at a specific spot within the text, enabling you to revisit it using a command or shortcut swiftly.

A position marker proves valuable when you shift your focus in the document to perform another action, such as cross-referencing information in a different section of text. Each document session allows for just one position marker; introducing a new marker erases any prior ones. When closing a document, its marker is also removed.

To accomplish this, navigate to Edit > Position Marker and consider the following actions:

- Position the insertion point within the text to insert a marker and then choose Insert Marker.
- For substituting an existing marker, choose Replace Marker.
- To eliminate a marker, opt for Remove Marker.
- To revisit a marker, select Go To Marker.

Reorder InCopy stories

Upon opening an assignments file or an InDesign document, you can rearrange the sequence of stories within the Galley or Story view. This reordering is fine with their layout positioning.

Follow these steps:

- Ensure you are in Galley or Story view.
- Drag the title of the story to your desired new location.

Recovery and Undo

Recover documents

InCopy protects your data in case of unexpected power or system failures through an automatic recovery function.

The automatically recovered data is stored in a temporary file, separate from the original document file on the disk. Typically, you won't have to concern yourself with the automatically recovered data, as any updates to the document stored in this recovery file will be seamlessly integrated into the original document file when you perform a Save or Save As action or when you exit InCopy. The automatically recovered data becomes significant only if you cannot successfully save your work before an unexpected power or system failure.

Despite these features, saving your files regularly and generating backup files is advisable to safeguard against unforeseen power or system failures.

Find recovered documents
Here are the steps to follow:

- Reboot your computer.
- Launch InCopy.
- If there's any automatically restored data, InCopy will show the retrieved document automatically. The term "[Recovered]" will be added after the filename in the document window's title bar, indicating the presence of unsaved modifications that were restored automatically.
- If InCopy crashes after attempting to open a document with automatically restored changes, the restored data might be damaged.
- Choose one of the following actions:
  1. For Adobe InCopy® files linked to an InDesign publication, pick File > Save.
  2. For standalone InCopy files, select File > Save As, define a location and a new filename, then click Save. This Save As function generates a new file incorporating the automatically restored data.

3. To discard any changes that were restored automatically and revert to the last saved version of the file, select File > Revert Content.

- Choose one of the following actions:

    1. To save the restored data, opt for File > Save As, select a location, specify a new filename, and click Save. The Save As operation preserves the restored version, including the automatically recovered data, and removes the "[Recovered]" label from the title bar.

    2. To disregard the changes that were automatically restored and utilize the most recent version of the document that was explicitly saved to the disk before the failure, close the file without saving and reopen the file from the disk, or select File > Revert.

Change the location of recovered documents.

- Navigate to Edit > Preferences > File Handling (Windows) or InCopy > Preferences > File Handling (Mac OS).
- Click Browse (Windows) or Choose (Mac OS) in the Document Recovery Data section.
- Indicate the desired location for the restored document, then select Select (Windows) or Choose (Mac OS), and conclude by clicking OK.

Undo mistakes

You can halt an ongoing lengthy process before its completion, reverse recent modifications, or revert to a previously saved state. You can reverse or redo numerous recent actions, typically up to a few hundred, although the count may be limited by available RAM and the types of actions performed. This series of actions is erased upon executing the Save As command, closing a document, or exiting the program.

Choose one of the following actions:

- To reverse the latest change, select Edit > Undo [action]. (Certain actions like scrolling cannot be undone.
- To redo an action, go to Edit > Redo [action].
- To undo all changes made since the last save of your project, pick File > Revert (InDesign) or File > Revert Content (InCopy).
- To dismiss a dialog box without applying any changes, click Cancel.

Customizing Preferences and Defaults

Settings encompassed within preferences involve aspects like the arrangement of panels, choices regarding measurements, and the display settings governing graphics and typography.

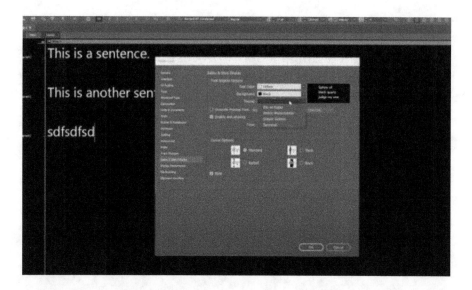

Preferences and defaults differ in their scope of application. Preference settings define how certain InCopy features should initially appear and function. Default settings, on the other hand, pertain to InCopy documents themselves.

Please take note: Preferences in InCopy can be fully automated through scripting. To ensure uniform preference settings across user groups, develop a script to configure these preferences and then have all users within the group run the script on their respective computers. Avoid directly copying and pasting one user's preference files onto another computer, which could lead to application instability.

Set defaults

Modifying settings without any open documents will establish new defaults for upcoming documents. Conversely, adjustments made to settings while a document is open will exclusively impact that particular document.

Similarly, altering settings when no objects are currently selected will define the defaults for new objects. To adjust default settings for fresh documents, follow these steps:

- Close all currently open documents.
- Modify menu items, panel configurations, or settings within dialog boxes as desired.

If you frequently employ the same page dimensions and language settings across multiple documents, you can redefine these defaults without having a document open. For instance, to modify the default page size, close all documents, navigate to File > Document Setup, and pick your desired page size. To establish a default dictionary, close all documents, go to Edit > Preferences > Dictionary (Windows) or InCopy > Preferences > Dictionary (Mac OS), and choose an option from the Language menu.

Specify default settings for new objects in a document

- While a document is active, select Edit > Deselect All.
- Adjust various menu items, panel configurations, or settings within dialog boxes.

To reset all preferences and default settings, perform one of the following actions:

- (For Windows) Launch InCopy, then simultaneously press Shift+Ctrl+Alt. Confirm deletion of preference files by clicking Yes when prompted.
- (For Mac OS) While holding down Shift+Option+Command+Control, start InCopy. Confirm deletion of preference files by clicking Yes in response to the prompt.

CHAPTER 2: INCOPY DOCUMENTS

Transforming Graphics

Position tool overview

Utilize the Position tool from the toolbox to manage chosen graphics, directly or in combination with a Transform command (Object > Transform), a command from a context menu, or keyboard shortcuts for nudging the graphic within its frame.

The Position tool is adaptable and alters its appearance based on different scenarios:

- When positioned above an empty graphics frame or a frame without content after using the File > Place command, it transforms into the loaded graphics icon, signifying the possibility of importing the graphic into that frame.
- Directly above a graphic, it transforms into the Hand tool, allowing selection and manipulation of the graphic within the frame.
- Hovering over the bounding box handle of an inline graphic causes it to morph into the resize arrow, indicating the potential to adjust the graphic's size through dragging.
- Above a graphics frame or the highest-level container of nested frames, it changes to the object select icon, denoting the capability to select the graphic or nested

frame beneath the cursor. The frame itself cannot be selected.

- When positioned over a text frame, it takes the form of an I-beam, signifying a text insertion point.

Set Position tool options

While employing the Position tool for relocating a graphic, you can hold the mouse button briefly to reveal a dynamic preview of the graphic (an image with a faint appearance) corresponding to any portion outside the frame. You can manage the appearance and timing of this preview.

Follow these steps:

- Double-click the Position tool located in the toolbox.
- From the Show Masked Portion of Image menu, choose the speed at which the complete image will emerge during dragging or opt to deactivate it entirely.

Transform graphics

You can use commands to move, scale, rotate, and shear graphics.

Move a graphic

Here are the steps to follow:

- Confirm that the frame containing the desired object is under your checkout, and then employ the Position tool to select the object.
- Navigate to Object > Transform > Move.

- Inside the Move dialog box, execute one of these actions:
- Input the horizontal and vertical distances for shifting the graphic. Positive values will move the object down and to the right of the x-axis, while negative values will shift it up and to the left.
- For precise movement of an object in terms of distance and angle, provide the required distance and angle values. The angle, measured in degrees from the x-axis, can be specified. Positive angles indicate a counterclockwise movement, while negative angles indicate a clockwise one. You can also insert values between 180° and 360°, which will be converted into their corresponding negative values (for example, a value of 270° becomes -90°).
- Choose one of the following:
  1. To preview the effect before applying it, opt for Preview.
  2. To execute the movement of the object, click OK.

Scale a graphic

1. Ensure that the frame containing the desired object is checked out to you, then use the Position tool to select the object.
2. Go to Object > Transform > Scale.
3. Within the Scale dialog box, ensure that the Constrain Proportions icon is activated if you wish to maintain the relative height and width of the object. Deactivate this icon if you intend to scale the X and Y values independently, which might lead to image distortion.

4. Enter the horizontal and vertical scale values as percentages (e.g., 90%) or distance values (e.g., 6p). Negative scale values are also acceptable.
5. Choose one of the following:
    - To preview the effect before applying it, choose Preview.
    - To apply the scaling, click OK.

Rotating an Object

- Confirm that the frame containing the desired object is under your checkout, then utilize the Position tool to select the object.
- Access Object > Transform > Rotate.
- Input the rotation angle in degrees within the Angle text box. To rotate the object clockwise, use a negative angle; for counterclockwise rotation, use a positive angle.
- Choose one of the following:
    1. To preview the effect before applying it, select Preview.
    2. To execute the rotation, click OK.

Shearing an Object

- Ensure that the frame containing the desired object is checked out to you, then utilize the Position tool to select the object.
- Choose Object > Transform > Shear.
- Inside the Shear dialog box, input the new shear angle. This angle determines the slant applied to the object with a line perpendicular to the shear axis. (Shear angle is calculated clockwise from the current axis.)

- Specify the axis along which the object will be sheared. It can be a horizontal, vertical, or angled axis.
- If an angled axis is chosen, input the desired axis angle in degrees relative to the perpendicular axis.
- Choose one of the following:
  1. To preview the effect before application, opt for Preview.
  2. To apply the shear transformation, click OK.

Stand-Alone Documents

Work with stand-alone documents.

An InCopy document not associated with an InDesign document is a stand-alone document. You can configure and adjust parameters such as the text area, page size, and orientation for these stand-alone documents. However, if the story later becomes linked to an InDesign document, the settings in InDesign will take precedence over those initially set in InCopy.

Please note: You also have the option to click "Save Preset" to store document settings for future usage. When generating a new document, you can directly select it from the Document Preset menu and proceed by clicking OK without needing to modify any settings. These stored presets can be shared among team members for collaborative editorial teams.

Create a stand-alone document.
- Navigate to File > New.

- To generate a document without facing pages in each spread, uncheck the option for Facing Pages.
- From the Text Area menu, opt for Frame Grid to produce a document with a grid designed for setting Japanese characters, or select Text Frame to create a standard text frame. (For more information on frame grids, refer to About frame grids in InCopy documents.)
- In the Text Area section, input values for Width and Depth. These text dimensions offer accurate line break information, eliminating the need to rely on InDesign for copyfit data.
- Specify whether the text direction should be horizontal or vertical. You can adjust this setting anytime by going to Type > Writing Direction > Horizontal or Vertical.
- Within the Grid Attributes section, define the characteristics of the frame grid, including vertical and horizontal scaling, character aki, and line aki. (For details on frame grid setup, consult Document setup options for frame grids.) These grid attributes won't appear when creating a plain text frame.
- Pick a page size from the options or input values for Width and Height. After trimming any bleeds or other marks outside the page, the chosen page size should represent the final dimensions.
- Click OK to proceed.

Opening a Stand-Alone Document

You can unveil an InCopy content file (.icml) that originates from either InCopy itself or emerges from the realm of InDesign. However, within the scope of InCopy, these InCopy content files diverge from revealing the page arrangement found within the InDesign document. Notably, you can access content from earlier versions of InCopy and even delve into InCopy template files (.icmt). Adding to this versatility, you hold the power to directly unfurl Microsoft® Word and text files right within InCopy, subsequently having the freedom to store them as either the stripped-down Text Only (.TXT) format or the more enriched Rich Text Format (.RTF).

- Venture to the File menu and choose Open.
- Handpick the document of your preference and unlock its contents by clicking Open. Alternatively, opt for File > Open Recent and select one of your recent projects. To tailor this experience, head to Edit > Preferences > File Handling (Windows) or InCopy > Preferences > File Handling and set the desired count for Number Of Recent Items To Display.

Creating a Document Layout

- Regardless of which vista of a standalone document you find yourself in, navigate to the File menu and select Document Setup.
- Within the ensuing dialog box, carve out the fundamental layout options.
- Finalize your design aspirations with a decisive click on OK to validate the changes.

Using Adobe Bridge with InCopy

Adobe Bridge is a versatile application packaged with various components of Adobe Creative Suite. Its role is to aid you in tracking down, arranging, and exploring the resources indispensable for crafting printed, online, video, and audio content. You can initiate Adobe Bridge from any Creative Suite module (except Adobe Acrobat) and harness its capabilities to access a diverse array of asset types, regardless of whether they belong to Adobe.

Within the realm of Adobe Bridge, you have the capacity to:

- Effectively manage image, footage, and audio files: Preview, search, categorize, and handle files directly within Adobe Bridge, bypassing the need to launch individual applications. You can also manipulate file metadata and deploy Adobe Bridge to seamlessly integrate files into your documents, projects, or compositions.
- Glimpse the links embedded within InDesign or InCopy documents in thumbnail form while operating in Adobe Bridge without actually opening the document itself.
- Engage in automated operations, including executing batch commands.
- Harmonize color settings across different color-managed Creative Suite modules.
- Initiate real-time web conferences to share your desktop and collaboratively review documents.

Browse for files by using Adobe Bridge.

Adobe Bridge enables you to effectively arrange, explore, and find the resources necessary to generate print, web, and mobile content. Select File > Browse In Bridge or click the Adobe Bridge icon in the application bar to access the Adobe Bridge Browser.

Saving and Exporting

Save documents

Choose one of the following actions:

1. To retain an existing document with the same name, go to File > Save Content.

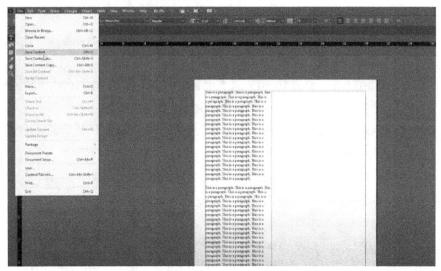

2. To keep a document under a new name, navigate to File > Save Content, indicate a location and filename, and press Save. The renamed document will be active.

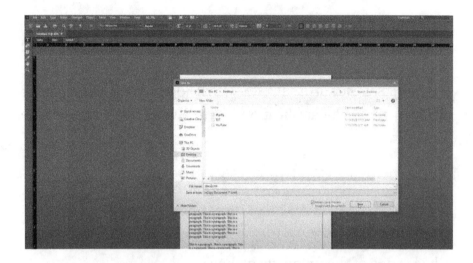

3. To duplicate a story or graphic under a different document name, pick File > Save Content Copy, specify a location and filename, and click Save. The duplicated version won't be the active document.

4. To generate a new document template from a copy, select File > Save Content As, choose a location and filename, and then opt for InCopy Template under Save As Type (Windows) or Format (Mac OS).

5. To save all stories in the document, select File > Save All Content.

6. To store a document as a text format copy, click on File > Save Content As, determine a location and filename, and then select either Text Only or Rich Text Format under Save As Type (Windows) or Format (Mac OS).

Note: When saving a managed (linked) document, the link in the InDesign file won't be updated. To update the story on the file system, follow the procedure outlined in your workflow system documentation or consult your system administrator.

Include previews in saved documents.

Thumbnail previews of files and templates in Adobe Bridge and Adobe Mini Bridge allow for convenient identification. These previews are generated when saving documents or templates. Document previews feature a JPEG image of the initial spread, while template previews display a JPEG image of each page. You can customize the preview size and number of pages as needed. For instance, selecting "Extra Large 1024x1024" permits detailed scanning of a page's content before opening the file.

You can activate this feature through Preferences or the Save As dialog. As previews augment file size and save time, you might enable this feature selectively through the Save As dialog when needed.

Follow these steps:

- Choose one of the following:
    1. To include a preview with every document saved, go to Edit > Preferences > File Handling (Windows) or InCopy > Preferences > File Handling (Mac OS).

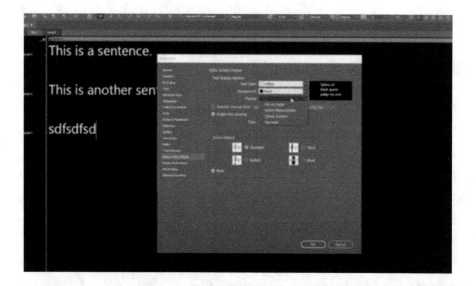

2. To add a preview for a specific document, select File > Save As.

3. To add a preview for a specific document, select File > Save Content As.

- Check the option "Always Save Preview Images With Documents."

- If you're adjusting the preview in Preferences, pick the number of preview pages from the Pages menu and choose an option from the Preview Size menu.

Note: Opting for the preview setting in the Save As dialog also applies the option in Preferences, along with the default Pages and Preview Size settings.

Export InCopy documents

You can save an entire InCopy document or specific parts in a different format. In most instances, each element within an

InCopy document, like text frames and graphics, is exported as separate files. However, exporting an InCopy document to Adobe PDF combines all text and graphics into a single PDF file.

Follow these steps:

- Choose one of the following actions:
    1. To export text, use the Type tool to click within the text.
    2. To export a graphic, click on the graphic using the Position tool.
- Go to File > Export.

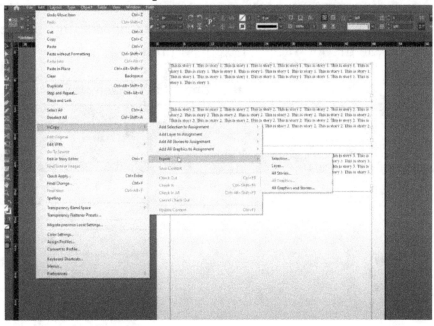

- Indicate a name and location for the exported content, then choose a format from the options under Save As Type.

  1. The XML format will only appear if the document contains XML tags.

  2. If you're exporting text and can't find an option for your word-processing application, you may need to use a format the application can import, such as Rich Text Format. If your word-processing application doesn't support any InCopy export formats, consider using the Text Only (ASCII) format.

  Exporting in ASCII format removes all character attributes from the text. To preserve formatting, utilize the InCopy Tagged Text export filter.

- Click Save to export the content in the selected format.

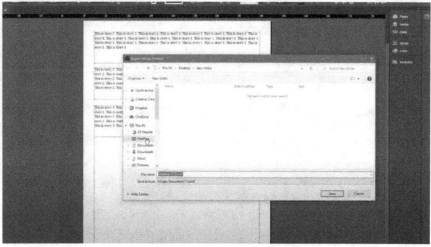

Rename InCopy stories

When exporting a story from InDesign, a document filename with a .icml extension is given. InCopy automatically uses this filename as the story name visible in the Assignments panel in InDesign and the story separator bar.

Unlike the filename, the story name is embedded within the file.

Here's how to manually change a story name:

- Open the story file in InCopy.
- Go to File > Content File Info.
- Ensure the Description tab is active, then input a new name under Document Title.

Depending on your system's workflow processes, an administrator might be required to modify your story name. If you encounter difficulties renaming the story as per the above steps, contact your workflow administrator.

Additionally, you can alter the story name in the Assignments panel while the story is checked out. However, the filename itself remains unchanged on the disk.

Export content to Buzzword

Buzzword is an online text editor that enables users to craft and store text files on a web server, and exporting a story to Buzzword results in creating a text file on the Buzzword server.

Follow these steps:

- Highlight the text or position the cursor within a text frame belonging to the desired story for export.
- Choose one of the following actions:
  1. In InDesign, go to File > Export For > Buzzword.
  2. In InCopy, select File > Export to Buzzword.
  3. If you still need to log into CS Live, click Sign In. Enter your email and password, then click Sign In.
- In the Export Story For Buzzword dialog box, designate the name for the upcoming Buzzword document and proceed by clicking OK.
- The resulting Buzzword document will open on Acrobat.com. You can relocate the document to a different workspace and easily share it with others.

Importing Graphics

Import graphics

InCopy permits the addition of graphics into pre-existing frames, which proves particularly advantageous when content is generated before layout design. This approach empowers you to select graphics for your articles as you write.

It's important to note that graphics can only be imported into existing frames. The creation of graphics frames is exclusive to InDesign users. Within standalone InCopy documents, graphics can be inserted into the default text frame, functioning as inline graphics.

InCopy supports various graphics file formats, mirroring InDesign's compatibility. It encompasses graphics produced using Adobe® Illustrator® 8.0 and beyond, bitmap formats like PDF, PSD, TIFF, GIF, JPEG, and BMP, and vector formats including EPS.

Furthermore, the capability to import InDesign (INDD) pages as images is present. Additional recognized formats include DCS, PICT, WMF, EMF, PCX, PNG, and Scitex CT (.SCT).

Notes on placing graphics in InCopy

When incorporating graphics into InCopy, remember the following points:

- For managed content, you must check out a frame before importing a graphic.
- After importing a graphic, you can manipulate it within the frame—moving, scaling, rotating, and shearing it. You can adjust the graphic to fit the frame and manage its appearance. You can also tag a frame for future XML usage through commands in the context menu.
- When InDesign users create a new frame, they indicate whether it's meant for text, graphics, or unassigned. However, InCopy users can't alter the frame type within InCopy. As a result, if you attempt to import a graphic into a text frame, it might appear oversized as an inline graphic.
- Graphics in InCopy can be selected and modified, but not the frames themselves unless they are nested or

inline frames. Altering graphics frames is exclusively possible for InDesign users.

- Insert graphics by placing, pasting, or dragging into anchored, floating, or inline frames. Importing graphics into a text frame is viable only if the frame possesses an active insertion point or is an inline graphics frame.

- Importing a graphic into a nested frame adds to the innermost frame beneath the pointer. Nested frames containing graphics can be chosen using the Position tool, which sets them apart from top-level frames.

- Effects like transparency, drop shadows, or feathering applied to a frame in InDesign remain visible in an InCopy assignment file or an open InDesign (.indd) file. However, they won't be visible in InCopy's linked (.icml) file.

Place a graphic in an InCopy document
Follow these steps:

- Choose one of the following actions:
    1. Position the cursor in the text frame to insert a graphic in an independent InCopy document.
    2. Ensure the graphics frame is checked out for a linked document. You'll see the Editing icon at the upper left corner of the frame.
- Go to File > Place and pick a graphics file.
- To configure specific import settings for the format, opt for Show Import Options. Once the format-specific settings are visible, click Open.

Note: When using the Show Import Options dialog for placing a graphic produced in Illustrator 9.0 or later, the options will match those for PDF files. If you're placing an Illustrator 8.x graphic, the options will resemble those for EPS files.

- If another dialog box emerges, choose your import preferences and click OK.
- To import into a frame, click on the graphics icon that's loaded into the frame. For inserting a designated page from a multipage PDF document, click on the loaded graphics icon within a frame.
- If you inadvertently replace an existing graphic with an image you're placing, press Ctrl+Z (Windows) or Command+Z (Mac OS) to revert to the original image within the frame and display the loaded graphics icon.

Drag a graphic into a frame
Choose one of the options below:

- If you wish to insert a graphic within an existing graphics frame, ensure that you have the frame checked out, and then drag the icon of the graphic file from your file system to the frame.
- To add a graphic at the current text insertion point, drag the icon of the graphic file to any location within the text frame. This approach is only applicable in the Layout view.

Paste a graphic into a frame

- Confirm that the graphics frame is under your checkout. The Editing icon will be visible in the upper left corner of the frame.
- Cut or copy a graphic.
- Hover the Hand tool above the graphics frame, right-click (Windows) or Control-click (Mac OS), and choose Paste Into.

To generate an inline graphic:

- Verify that you check out the text frame. The Editing icon will be displayed in the upper left corner of the frame.
- Choose one of the following actions.
  1. For inserting a graphic within an existing inline graphics frame, use the Place or Cut command to select a graphic. Click on the loaded graphics icon within the frame.
  2. To insert a graphic at the active text insertion point, drag the icon of the graphic file to any location within the text frame. Alternatively, employ the Place command to import the graphic.

Controlling Graphics Display

Control graphics' display performance

You can manage the resolution of graphics you incorporate into your document. You can adjust the display preferences for the entire document or specific graphics. Additionally, you can modify a setting allowing the option to follow or disregard display preferences per document.

Change a document's display performance

Upon opening, a document will consistently adopt the default Display Performance settings. While a document is open, you can modify its display performance, although this change won't be preserved when saving it. If you've set different display performances for individual images, you can unify the settings for all objects.

Follow these steps:

- Opt for View > Layout View.
- Navigate to View > Display Performance and pick an option from the provided submenu.
- To enforce the document's display setting on objects you've configured individually, uncheck View > Display Performance > Allow Object-Level Display Settings. (A checkmark indicates that it's currently selected.)

Change an object's display performance

Follow these instructions:

- Opt for View > Layout View.
- To maintain the display performance settings for individual objects even after closing and reopening the document, ensure that Preserve Object-Level Display Settings are checked within the Display Performance preferences.

- Navigate to View > Display Performance and ensure that Allow Object-Level Display Settings are selected.
- Use either the Selection or Direct Selection tools to choose an imported graphic.
- Employ the Position tool to select an imported graphic.
- Choose one of the following actions:
    1. Select Object > Display Performance and pick a desired display setting.
    2. Right-click (Windows) or Control-click (Mac OS) on the image, then select a display setting from the Display Performance submenu.
- To eliminate a specific object's customized display setting, select Use View Setting within the Display Performance submenu. If you want to remove custom display settings for all graphics in the document, opt for Clear Object-Level Display Settings within the View > Display Performance submenu.

Display performance options

These choices manage the visual representation of graphics on the screen, but they don't impact the quality of prints or exported content.

- **Utilize Display:** Performance preferences to establish the default option for opening all documents and customize the settings defining those choices. Each display option has distinct settings for showing raster images, vector graphics, and transparencies.
- **Fast:** Depicts a raster image or vector graphic as a gray box (default). This choice is suitable for rapidly

navigating through spreads with numerous images or transparency effects.

- **Typical:** Displays a low-resolution proxy image (default) suitable for identifying and placing images or vector graphics. It is the default and quickest method to view a recognizable image.
- **High Quality:** Shows a raster image or vector graphic in High Resolution (default). This option offers superior quality but operates at a slower pace. Opt for this when you need to fine-tune an image meticulously.

Customize the display performance options

You can personalize the definitions for each display performance choice (Fast, Typical, and High Quality). Each option has distinct settings for raster (bitmap) images, vector graphics, and transparency effects.

For managed (linked) InCopy stories, lower-resolution proxy data is included for images. It avoids downloading the full-resolution image from the server whenever the file is checked out.

Here's how to do it:

- Choose Edit > Preferences > Display Performance (Windows) or InCopy > Preferences > Display Performance (Mac OS).

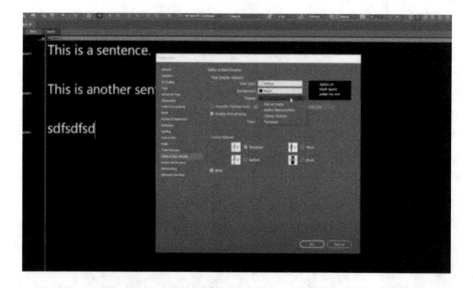

- Under Adjust View Settings, pick the display option you want to customize.
- For each display option, adjust the sliders for Raster Images or Vector Graphics according to your preference:
    1. **Gray Out:** Represents an image as a gray box.
    2. **Proxy:** Displays images at proxy resolution (72 dpi).
    3. **High Resolution:** Exhibits images at the maximum resolution supported by the monitor and current view settings.
- For each display option, modify the Transparency slider as desired:
    1. **Off:** Transparency effects aren't shown.
    2. **Low Quality:** Basic transparency (opacity and blend modes) is displayed, while transparency effects (drop shadow and feather) appear as low-resolution approximations.

3. **Medium Quality:** Shows low-resolution drop shadows and feathers. This mode is suitable for most tasks unless the document is rich in transparency or contains numerous transparency effects.

4. **High Quality:** Presents higher-resolution (144 dpi) drop shadows and feathers, CMYK mattes, and isolated spreads.

Note: In documents where blending is set to CMYK and overprint preview or soft proofing is active, opacity matting occurs in CMYK instead of RGB. It means semi-transparent CMYK colors display as tinted CMYK colors.

- To enable anti-aliasing for text, stroke, fill, and other page elements, select Enable Anti-aliasing. The resulting outlines can be anti-aliased if the text is converted to outlines (Mac OS only).
- To determine the point size at which text displays as a faded bar, input a value for Greek Type Below.
- Click OK.
- To restore all settings to the original defaults, click Use Defaults.

CHAPTER 3: TEXT

Adding Text

Text can be included through typing, pasting, or importing from another file in InCopy. Regular word-processing methods are applied when working with text in InCopy. Use the Type tool in the toolbox and follow the approaches mentioned below.

These techniques function similarly in Galley, Story, and Layout views, regardless of whether the content is connected to Adobe InDesign®.

- **For Typing:** Position the insertion point where you wish to insert text and start typing.
- **For Selection:** Employ dragging, double-clicking, or triple-clicking to choose individual characters, words, lines, or paragraphs (based on the Preferences settings). Alternatively, click anywhere in the content and opt for Edit > Select All.
- **For Pasting:** Copy or cut text, click the desired spot, and choose Edit > Paste. To eliminate the formatting of the pasted content, go for Edit > Paste Without Formatting. To manage spacing, choose Adjust Spacing Automatically When Cutting And Pasting Words in the Type section of the Preferences dialog box.

To retain font, font size, and character spacing settings from copied text, use Edit > Paste Without Grid Format to paste into a frame grid.

- **For Deletion:** Pick the text you want to remove, and select Edit > Clear.
  Additionally, you can directly import text from another text document.

Importing files

Text can be brought in from sources like other InCopy stories, Microsoft® Word, Microsoft Excel, and applications capable of exporting text in Rich Text Format (RTF) or plain text. All these importable file formats are listed in the InCopy Place dialog box (under the Files Of Type menu for Windows® and in the right list pane for Mac OS).

Regarding document formatting and styles, you can import files with or without formatting. If you choose to import files with formatting, InCopy incorporates most character and paragraph formatting attributes from text files. However, it disregards page layout details such as page breaks, margins, and column settings (which can be set in InDesign). In general, InCopy imports all formatting details specified in the word-processing application, except for features not supported in InCopy.

When an import filter exists for an application, you can decide which styles to import and which formatting to apply in case of name conflicts.

Keep in mind that InDesign manages styles in linked InCopy stories. Placing an InCopy story in InDesign leads to imported styles in the InCopy document being overridden in InDesign if there are style name conflicts.

When saving files for import, if your word-processing application offers multiple file formats, it's advisable to choose the one that retains the most formatting—either the native file format of the application or an interchange format like Rich Text Format (RTF).

Recent versions of Microsoft Word files can be imported. If you're dealing with files from older word-processing applications or Word 95 for Windows and earlier (e.g., Word 6), open them in their original application and save them in a compatible Word format or in RTF to preserve most formatting.

Place (import) text

The Place command is the most effective method to import substantial amounts of text. InCopy provides support for a range of formats, encompassing word processing, spreadsheets, and text files. The extent to which the initial formatting remains intact relies on the file type's import filter and the choices made during the placement process. Word, text, and RTF files can be directly opened in InCopy.

Click where you want the text to appear to add text using the Type tool. Follow these steps:

- Go to File > Place.

- In the Place dialog box, you can display import options by selecting "Show Import Options" if desired.

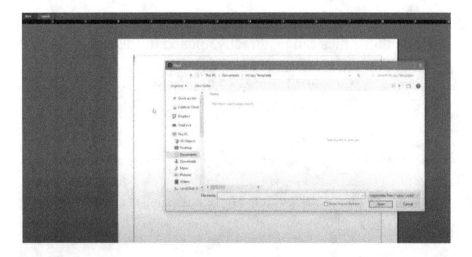

- Choose the desired text file for placement and click Open. If you Shift-click Open, the Import Options dialog box appears even if "Show Import Options" is not selected.

You can perform the following actions:

- If the import options dialog displays for the file type you're placing, select the desired options and click OK.
- If the document you're importing contains fonts unavailable on your system, a dialog box will notify you of font substitutions. If you wish to specify alternative fonts for substitution, click "Find Font" and make your choices.

If the imported text includes highlighting in colors like pink or green, specific composition preference options are likely enabled. To address this, navigate to the Composition section of the Preferences dialog box and review the settings under Highlight. For instance, text formatted with fonts not present in InCopy might be highlighted in pink.

Import options

When you import Word, Excel, and tagged text files, you can determine how the files are imported.

Microsoft Word and RTF import options

When you decide to reveal the import options while placing a Word or RTF file, you can choose from the following alternatives:

- **Table Of Contents Text:** Brings in the table of contents as text within the story. These entries are imported solely as text.
- **Index Text:** Imports the index as text within the story. These entries are also imported as text only.
- **Footnotes:** Imports Word footnotes, preserving content while renumbering based on the document's footnote settings. If Word footnotes aren't imported correctly, consider saving the Word document in RTF format and importing the RTF file.
- **Endnotes:** Imports endnotes as part of the text at the story's end.
- **Use Typographer's Quotes:** Ensures imported text employs proper left and right quotation marks ("") and apostrophes (') instead of straight marks ("") and apostrophes (').
- **Remove Styles And Formatting From Text And Tables:** Eliminates formatting, like typeface, color, and style, from the imported text, including table content.

This option excludes paragraph styles and inline graphics during import.

- **Preserve Local Overrides:** When formatting is stripped but local character formatting (e.g., bold, italics) exists within a paragraph, this maintains those character attributes. Deselecting this option removes all formatting.
- **Convert Tables:** When formatting is removed, tables can be converted to basic, unformatted tables or unformatted, tab-delimited text.
- **Preserve Styles And Formatting From Text And Tables:** Maintains the Word document's formatting in InDesign or InCopy, with further options in the Formatting section for specific preservation.
- **Manual Page Breaks:** How Word's page breaks are adapted in InDesign or InCopy. Choose between preserving, converting to column breaks, or having no breaks.
- **Import Inline Graphics:** Keeps inline graphics from the Word document in InCopy.
- **Import Unused Styles:** Imports all Word document styles, regardless of their application.
- **Convert Bullets & Numbers To Text:** Imports bullets and numbers as actual characters to maintain paragraph appearance. Note that numbers in numbered lists may not automatically update when list items change.

- **Track Changes:** Incorporates Track Changes markups from Word into InCopy, viewable in InDesign's Story Editor.
- **Import Styles Automatically:** Transfers styles from the Word document into the InDesign or InCopy document, with options to resolve style conflicts.
- **Customize Style Import:** Enables the Style Mapping dialog box to specify which InCopy style corresponds to each Word style in the imported document.
- **Save Preset:** Stores current Word Import Options for later use. You can select the preset you've created when importing Word styles again.

InCopy transforms paragraph and character styles but not bulleted and numbered list styles.

Text-file import options

When you opt to display the import options while placing a text file, you have the following choices available:

- **Character Set:** Designates the character set used in the text file, like ANSI, Unicode UTF8, Shift JIS, or Chinese Big 5. The default selection corresponds to the default language and platform of InDesign or InCopy.
- **Platform:** Specifies whether the file was generated in Windows or Mac OS.
- **Set Dictionary To:** Specifies the Dictionary to apply to the imported text.
- **Extra Carriage Returns:** Defines the handling of additional paragraph returns during import. Select

between options like "Remove At End Of Every Line" or "Remove Between Paragraphs."

- **Replace:** Substitutes a defined number of spaces with a tab.
- **Use Typographer's Quotes:** Ensures that imported text integrates proper left and right quotation marks ("") and apostrophes (') instead of straight marks ("") and apostrophes (').

Microsoft Excel import options

When importing an Excel file, you can select from these choices:

- **Sheet:** Indicates the specific worksheet to import.
- **View:** Determines whether to import stored custom or personal views or to disregard them.
- **Cell Range:** Specifies the cell range to import using a colon (:) to indicate the range (e.g., A1:G15). If named ranges exist within the worksheet, they will be listed in the Cell Range menu.
- **Import Hidden Cells Not Saved In View:** Encompasses cells formatted as hidden cells in the Excel spreadsheet.
- **Table:** Decides the presentation of the spreadsheet data in the document.
  1. **Formatted Table:** InCopy aims to retain the same Excel formatting, although cell text formatting might need to be completely preserved. Updating the link when the spreadsheet is linked rather than

embedded will override any InCopy table formatting.

2. **Unformatted Table:** Imports the table without formatting from the spreadsheet. You can apply a table style to the imported table. Formatting applied using paragraph and character styles is preserved even when updating the link.

3. **Unformatted Tabbed Text:** Imports the table as tab-delimited text, which can be converted into a table in InDesign or InCopy.

4. **Formatted Only Once:** InDesign maintains initial Excel formatting upon import. For linked spreadsheets, formatting changes made are disregarded in the linked table during updates. This option isn't available in InCopy.

- **Table Style:** Applies a specified table style to the imported content. It is applicable only if "Unformatted Table" is chosen.
- **Cell Alignment:** Determines cell alignment in the imported document.
- **Include Inline Graphics:** Retains inline graphics from the Excel file in InCopy.
- **Number Of Decimal Places To Include:** Defines the decimal places for spreadsheet figures.
- **Use Typographer's Quotes:** Ensures imported text contains proper left and right quotation marks ("") and

apostrophes (') rather than straight marks ("") and apostrophes (').

Tagged-text import options

You can utilize the tagged text format to import (or export) a text file that can leverage InCopy's formatting capabilities. Tagged-text files are text documents that include information describing the desired formatting for InCopy. Properly tagged text can encompass nearly every aspect of an InCopy story, encompassing attributes at both the paragraph and character levels and special characters.

When importing a tagged-text file and selecting "Show Import Options" in the Place dialog box, the following choices are at your disposal:

- **Use Typographer's Quotes:** Ensures that imported text incorporates appropriate left and right quotation marks ("") and apostrophes (') rather than straight marks ("") and apostrophes (').
- **Remove Text Formatting:** Eliminates the imported text's formatting, such as typeface, color, and style.
- **Resolve Text Style Conflicts Using:** Specify which character or paragraph style to apply when a conflict arises between the style in the tagged-text file and the style in the InDesign document. You can select "Publication Definition" to utilize the existing definition for that style in InDesign or "Tagged File Definition" to apply the style defined in the tagged text.

- **Show List Of Problem Tags Before Place:** Presents an inventory of unrecognized tags. If this list emerges, you can proceed with the import or cancel it. In case of continuation, the file might appear differently than anticipated.

Import Buzzword documents

Buzzword is an online text editor that enables users to generate and store text files on a web server. In InCopy CS5, importing and exporting text to and from Buzzword documents is possible.

When you import a Buzzword document, a URL-linked connection is established to the document on the server. If changes are made to the Buzzword document externally, you can employ the Links panel in InCopy to update the imported version. However, this process eliminates any alterations you've made to the Buzzword text within InCopy.

Keep in mind that the Buzzword application in Acrobat.com is accessible in English, French, and German languages.

Here's how to proceed:

- Go to File > Place From Buzzword.

- If you're not logged into CS Live, click Sign In, provide your email and password, and then click Sign In.
- After signing in, the Place Buzzword Documents dialog box will showcase a list of Buzzword documents available for import.
- Choose the desired documents for import, or insert the URL of the Buzzword document into the Paste URL field.
- Select any of the following options and click OK:
    1. **Show Import Options:** If chosen, the Buzzword Import Options dialog box appears before placing the file.
    2. **Replace Selected Item:** Opt for this to replace the currently selected object in the document.
    3. **Link To Document:** Select this to establish a link between the Buzzword document and the placed text. Updates to the Buzzword document

are indicated in the Links panel. Link updates will refresh the text in InCopy, though formatting changes applied in InCopy will be lost.

- **Apply Grid Format:** Reformat the imported text based on grid attributes.
- If you've chosen "Show Import Options," you can define settings within the Buzzword Import Options dialog box. This dialog box shares many options with the RTF Import Options dialog box.
- Create a text frame by clicking or dragging with the text cursor active.

Type Asian text using inline input

- Opt for Edit > Preferences > Advanced Type (Windows) or InCopy > Preferences > Advanced Type (Mac OS) from the menu.

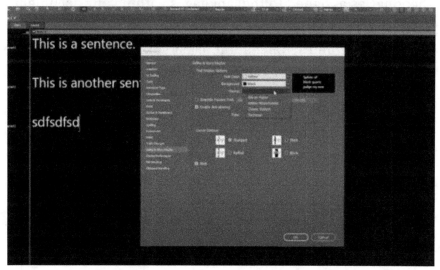

- Mark the option for Using Inline Input for Non-Latin Text, and press OK.

Utilize a system input method, when accessible, to include 2-byte and 4-byte characters, which proves particularly handy for inputting Asian characters. Additionally, a dedicated input program enables direct input of Asian text into text frames.

Checking Spelling

You can verify the correctness of the language used in a document or across various open stories. InCopy highlights words misspelled or unfamiliar, instances of repeated words (like "the the"), words that lack capitalization, and sentences that lack capitalization. InCopy scrutinizes all XML content and expands inline notes during the spell-check process.

When you engage in spell check, InCopy refers to the dictionaries assigned to the languages within your document's text. InCopy employs the Proximity language dictionaries for both spelling and hyphenation, each containing an extensive array of words with standardized hyphenation patterns.

For self-contained stories (stories that aren't linked to an InDesign layout), you can tailor the language dictionaries to ensure proper recognition of unique vocabulary. For instance, during a spelling check (Edit > Spelling > Check Spelling), you can click the "Add" button and input your preferred settings.

To configure spelling preferences

- Access Edit > Preferences > Spelling (Windows) or InCopy > Preferences > Spelling (Mac OS).

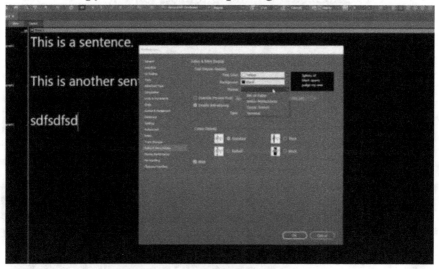

- Choose from the following options:
    1. Select "Misspelled Words" to identify words not found in the language dictionary.
    2. Choose "Repeated Words" to detect duplicate words like "the the."
    3. Opt for "Uncapitalized Words" to locate words (e.g., "germany") only present in lowercase in the dictionary, though they should be capitalized (e.g., "Germany").
    4. Select "Uncapitalized Sentences" to identify words not capitalized after periods, exclamation marks, and question marks.

- Enable "Dynamic Spelling" to underline potentially misspelled words while typing.
- Specify the underlined color for misspelled, repeated, uncapitalized, and uncapitalized sentences.

To initiate a spell check

- Designate the language using the Language menu in the Character panel if the document contains foreign-language text.
- Navigate to Edit > Spelling > Check Spelling to initiate the spell-check process.

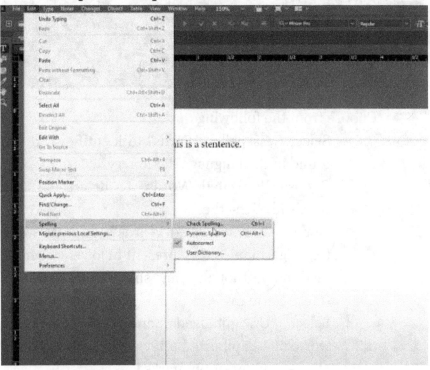

- Throughout the process, when unfamiliar words, misspellings, or potential errors arise, you have various options:

  1. Click "Skip" to proceed with spell-checking without altering the highlighted word.

  2. Select "Ignore All" to disregard all instances of the highlighted word until InCopy is restarted.

  3. Choose a correction from the "Suggested Corrections" list or input the correct word in the "Change To" box, then click "Change" to modify only that instance of the misspelled word. Alternatively, click "Change All" to modify all occurrences throughout the document. To add a word to the dictionary, pick the appropriate dictionary from the "Add To" menu and click "Add."

  4. Click "Dictionary" to open the Dictionary dialog box, where you can specify the added word's target dictionary, language, and hyphenation breaks. For addition to all languages, select "All Languages" from the Language menu and click "Add."

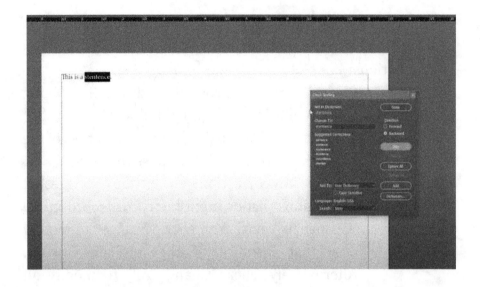

Correct spelling errors as you type

Enabling Autocorrect allows for the automatic replacement of capitalization errors and frequently made typing mistakes as you type. Before utilizing Autocorrect, it's necessary to compile a roster of commonly misspelled words and link them to their accurate spellings.

Here's how to set up Autocorrect:

- Access Edit > Preferences > Autocorrect (Windows) or InCopy > Preferences > Autocorrect (Mac OS).

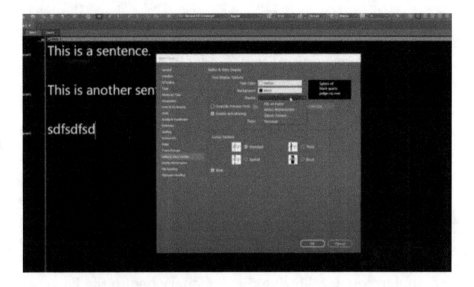

- Opt for "Enable Autocorrect." (You can also toggle this feature on or off swiftly by using Edit > Spelling > Autocorrect.)
- Select the language for which the autocorrections should apply from the Language menu.
- To rectify capitalization errors (e.g., typing "germany" instead of "Germany"), mark "Autocorrect Capitalization Errors." You don't need to include capitalized words in the autocorrection list.
- To add a commonly misspelled word, click "Add," input the misspelled term (e.g., "teh"), correct (e.g., "the"), and then confirm with "OK."
- Repeat this process for other frequently misspelled words, and finalize by clicking "OK."

Whenever you type any of the words you've included in the list of misspelled words, the word will automatically be replaced with the correction you provided.

To manage your autocorrect list:

1. To remove a word you've added, select it from the list and choose "Remove."
2. To modify autocorrect words, select the word, click "Edit," make the necessary corrections, and confirm with "OK."

Use dynamic spelling

You can rectify spelling mistakes via the context menu when dynamic spelling is activated. Words that might be misspelled are underscored, following the dictionary tied to the language of the text. If you're typing in various languages, ensure the correct language is assigned to the selected text.

Here's how to make use of dynamic spelling:

- To enable dynamic spelling, opt for Edit > Spelling > Dynamic Spelling.

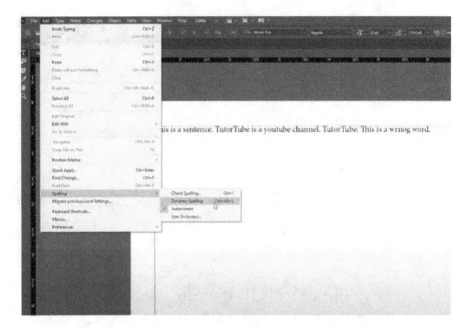

1. Words that could be misspelled will be underlined within your document.

2. Right-click (Windows) or Control-click (Mac OS) on the underlined word, and then choose from the following actions:

3. Select a suggested correction. For repeated words or words requiring capitalization, options include "Delete Repeated Word [word]" or "Capitalize [word]."

- Choose "Add [word] To User Dictionary." It will incorporate the word into the current dictionary without opening the dialog box. The word remains unchanged in the text.

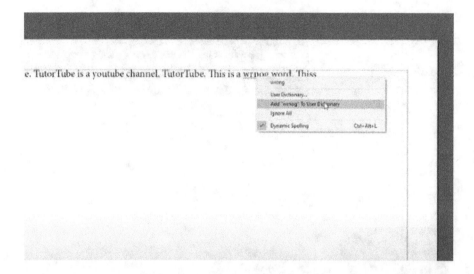

- Click "Dictionary." This action opens the Dictionary dialog box, enabling you to choose the Target dictionary, adjust hyphenation breaks, and specify a language. Select "All Languages" from the Language menu to include the word in all languages and click "Add." The word is integrated into the selected dictionary and remains unaltered in the text.

  1. Select "Ignore All" to dismiss instances of this word across all documents. Upon restarting InCopy, the word will be flagged again as a potential misspelling.

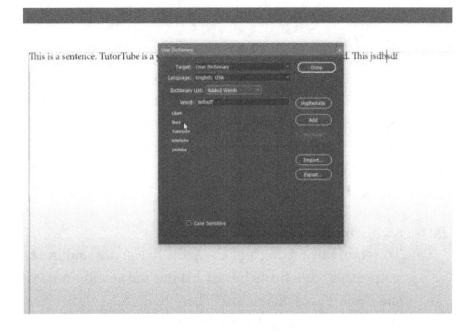

If you've selected "Ignore All" and later decide to reverse that decision, navigate to the Dictionary dialog box, choose "Ignored Words" from the Dictionary List menu, and remove the word.

Editing Text

Paste text

You have the option to insert text from another software or Adobe InCopy.

When you paste text into InDesign and the insertion point isn't within a text frame, a new simple text frame will be generated. On the other hand, if the insertion point is located inside a text frame, the text will be inserted into that specific frame. If you've highlighted text before pasting, the pasted text will overwrite the selected text.

Utilizing "Edit > Paste Without Grid Format" to insert text into a frame grid allows the pasted text to maintain its original font, font size, and character spacing settings from the copied text. If you apply grid formatting to the pasted text, you can select the text and use "Edit > Apply Grid Format" to align it with the character attributes of the frame grid.

Paste text from another application

- To retain formatting and elements like styles and index markers, access the Clipboard Handling section within the Preferences dialog box. Then, pick "All Information" under the Paste set. To exclude these elements and formatting during pasting, opt for "Text Only."
- Cut or copy the desired text within a different application or from an InCopy document.
- You can optionally select the text or click inside a text frame. Otherwise, the text will be inserted into its new frame.
- Choose one of the following actions:
    1. Select Edit > Paste. If the pasted text lacks specific formatting, you might need to adjust the Import Options dialog box settings for RTF documents.
    2. Opt for Edit > Paste Without Formatting. (This option will be inactive if you paste text from

another application while "Text Only" is chosen in Clipboard Handling Preferences.)

3. Choose Edit > Paste Without Grid Format.

Adjust spacing automatically when pasting text

When text is pasted, spaces might be added or eliminated automatically based on the context. For instance, when a word is cut and then pasted between two words, spaces will be inserted before and after the word. However, a space won't be added if you paste the word before a period at the end of a sentence.

Here's how to set this up:

- Navigate to Edit > Preferences > Type (Windows) or InCopy > Preferences > Type (Mac OS).

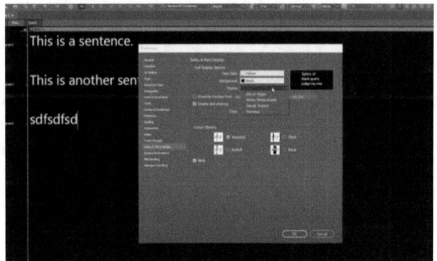

- Choose "Enable Automatic Spacing Adjustment When Cutting and Pasting Words," then confirm by clicking OK.

Paste text to a frame grid

You can insert text while maintaining its original formatting from the source. If you copy text with altered attributes from one frame grid and paste it into a different one, only those modified attributes will be retained. Alternatively, you can paste the text without adhering to grid formatting.

Here's how to do it:

- Cut or copy the desired text within another application or an InCopy document.
- Position the text insertion point within the frame grid or highlight a portion of the text.
- Choose one of the following actions:
    1. To paste text that conforms to the grid format, select Edit > Paste.
    2. Opt for Edit > Paste Without Grid Format to paste text without applying grid formatting.

You always have the option to apply grid formatting afterward by selecting Edit > Apply Grid Format. The grid format attributes defined in the Named Grids panel will be implemented into the text.

Apply grid format to text

You can implement the grid format onto any text that doesn't adhere to it.

- Highlight the text.
- Opt for Edit > Apply Grid Format.

Change the text direction

- Pick the text frame.
- Take either of these actions:
    1. Go to Type > Writing Direction > Horizontal or Vertical.
    2. Navigate to Type > Story to access the Story panel. Choose either Horizontal or Vertical for Story Direction.
- In the Galley view or Story view, the text will appear horizontal, regardless of whether Vertical is selected. However, the text will be vertical if Vertical is chosen in Layout View.
- Switching from a vertical text frame or frame grid to a horizontal one, or vice versa, results in a conversion. This modification impacts the entire story and affects all frames linked to the selected ones.

Drag and drop text

You can use the mouse to drag and drop text in the Story Editor or Layout View. You can also move text from the Story Editor to the layout window (or vice versa) and even into certain dialog boxes like Find/Change. It's important to note that dragging text from a locked or checked-in story will copy the text instead of moving it. Additionally, you can copy text or create a new frame while dragging and dropping text.

You can similarly use the mouse to drag and drop text in Galley View, Story View, or Layout View, and you can even drag text into specific dialog boxes such as Find/Change. Like the earlier description, dragging text from a locked or checked-in story will copy it, not move it. You can also copy text during the dragging process.

Jeff Witchel provides a video tutorial about this drag-and-drop functionality in a resource named "Using InDesign Drag and Drop Text."

Here's how to enable drag and drop:

- Access Edit > Preferences > Type (Windows) or InCopy > Preferences > Type (Mac OS). Then, select "Enable In Layout View," "Enable In Story Editor (InDesign)," or "Enable In Galley/Story View (InCopy)," and confirm with OK.

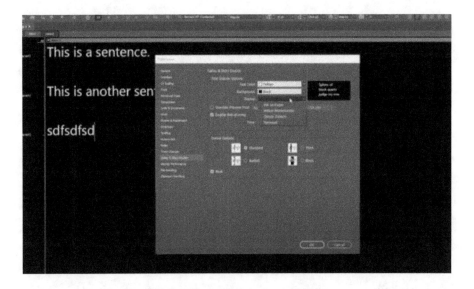

- Highlight the text you wish to either move or copy.
- Hover the pointer over the selected text until the drag and drop icon appears ( ), then initiate the drag by moving the text.
- While dragging, the selected text will remain in its original location, but a vertical bar will indicate where the text will be placed upon releasing the mouse button. This vertical bar will appear within any text frame dragged over by the mouse.
- Take any of these actions:
    1. To place the text in a new position, position the vertical bar where the text appears and release the mouse button.
    2. To place the text in a new frame, hold down Ctrl (Windows) or Command (Mac OS) after starting the drag, then release the mouse button before releasing the key.

3. To drop the text without retaining formatting, hold down Shift after beginning the drag, then release the mouse button before releasing the key.

4. To copy the text, hold down Alt (Windows) or Option (Mac OS) after beginning the drag, then release the mouse button before releasing the key.

Transpose characters

Should you inadvertently switch the positions of two neighboring characters while typing, you can rectify this using the Transpose command. For instance, if you entered 1243 instead of 1234, the Transpose command will effectively swap the 4 and the 3 positions.

Here's how to go about it:

- Position the insertion point between the two characters that require transposing.
- Opt for Edit > Transpose.

Edit text on a parent page

Within InDesign documents, a parent page is a template that impacts multiple pages. Parent pages mainly dictate common layout elements visible across all document pages, like margins, page numbers, headers, and footers. If the text on an InDesign parent page is linked, you can use InCopy to edit that text.

Nonetheless, altering frame attributes controlled by the parent isn't possible, and you can't edit parent-page text from regular pages elsewhere in the document.

If you can't place an insertion point into a nonlocked text frame on a regular page, it could be because that text is on a parent page. In such cases, it's advisable to consult the individuals who established the frames and your design team for clarification.

Here's how to work with this in InDesign:

1. If your document still needs to be added to Layout View, choose View > Layout View.
2. Select the parent page From the page box in the document window's lower left corner.

3. On the parent page, highlight the text you wish to modify and proceed to make your changes.

Remember that for editing text on a parent page, the parent page must incorporate managed stories currently checked out.

Undo actions

You can undo or redo several hundred of the most recent actions. The exact number of actions you can undo is limited by the amount of RAM available and the kinds of actions you have performed. The record of recent actions is erased when you save, close, quit, or exit, so they can no longer be undone. You can cancel an operation or revert to a previously saved version before it completes.

Do one of the following:

- Choose Edit > Undo [action] to undo the most recent change. (You cannot undo specific actions, such as scrolling.)
- To redo an action you just undid, choose Edit > Redo [action].
- To undo all changes made since the last time you saved the project, choose File > Revert Content.
- Press the Escape key to stop a change that InCopy hasn't finished processing (for example, if you see a progress bar).
- To close a dialog box without applying changes, click Cancel.

Find/Change

Find and change text

When seeking to create a list, locate, or substitute fonts within your document, you may find it more suitable to utilize the Find Font command instead of the Find/Change command.

Find and change text
- To search within a specific text range or story, highlight the text or position the insertion point within the story.

For searches across multiple documents, open those documents.

- Click Edit > Find/Change and then access the Text tab.
- Define the scope of your search using the Search menu, and utilize icons to encompass locked layers, master pages, footnotes, and other elements in the search.
- In the Find What box, describe the content you're looking for:
    1. Input or paste the desired text to find.
    2. Select a representative character (metacharacter) from the menu beside the Find What box to locate or replace tabs, spaces, or special characters. You can also opt for wildcard choices like Any Digit or Any Character.
    3. Employ predefined queries for finding and replacing text.
- In the Change To box, input or paste the replacement text. You can choose a representative character from the menu next to the Change To box.
- Click Find.
- To continue searching, utilize options like Find Next, Change (to modify the current occurrence), Change All (which displays the total changes made), or Change/Find (to alter the current occurrence and locate the next one).
- Click Done.
- If your search doesn't yield the expected outcomes, verify if there's any formatting applied from a previous search. You should also broaden your search by checking

if you're only searching within a selection or a story instead of the entire document. The text you're searching for is associated with an item like a locked layer, footnote, or concealed conditional text, which might be excluded from the search.

- You can use Edit > Undo Replace Text (or Undo Replace All Text) if you decide to reverse the text replacements.
- To swiftly find the subsequent instance of a previously searched-for phrase without opening the Find/Change dialog box, you can use Edit > Find Next. Moreover, previously used search strings are stored in the Find/Change dialog box, allowing you to select a search string from the menu next to the respective option.

Find and change formatted text

- Choose Edit > Find/Change.
- If the Find Format and Change Format options don't appear, click More Options.
- Click the Find Format box or the Specify Attributes To Find icon to the right of the Find Format Settings section.
- On the left side of the Find Format Settings dialog box, select a type of formatting, specify the format attributes, and click OK.
- Some OpenType formatting options appear in both the OpenType Options and Basic Character Formats (Position menu) sections. For information on OpenType and other formatting attributes, search for the related topic in InCopy Help.

- To search for (or replace with) formatting only, leave the Find What or Change To box blank.
- If you want to apply formatting to the text found, click the Change Format box or the Specify Attributes To Change icon in the Change Format Settings section. Then, select a type of formatting, specify the format attributes, and click OK.
- Use the Find and Change buttons to format the text. If you specify formatting for your search criteria, info icons appear above the Find What or Change To boxes. These icons indicate that formatting attributes have been set, and the find or change operation will be restricted accordingly.

CONCLUSION

A dobe InCopy is a robust word-processing solution that proves indispensable for individuals involved in writing, editing, and design, offering a streamlined workflow and heightened productivity. Throughout this guide, we've delved into the vast functionalities inherent to InCopy. It spans from establishing and utilizing InCopy workflows to applying formatting styles and fine-tuning line and page divisions.

Throughout this resource, we've furnished tangible instances and systematic guidelines to empower you in mastering InCopy and elevating your efficiency and efficacy.

InCopy facilitates real-time collaboration, formatting style implementation, line and page adjustment, and other features. Whether you find yourself in the role of a writer, editor, or designer, InCopy is replete with tools to facilitate the creation and editing of documents with unparalleled ease.

Our aspiration is that this guide serves as a valuable reference, equipping you to unlock the complete potential of Adobe InCopy. We express our gratitude for accompanying us on this journey and extend our best wishes for your future undertakings.

www.ingramcontent.com/pod-product-compliance
Lightning Source LLC
LaVergne TN
LVHW051536050326
832903LV00033B/4268